GOD
Will Always Be There For You

a Daily Guide to
Christian Inspirational Living

ROBERT MOMENT

LEGAL STATEMENT

© Copyright 2009 by Robert Moment. All rights reserved.

No part of this book may be used or reproduced in any manner without the express written permission of the author.

ISBN-13: 978-0-9799982-0-1   ISBN-10: 0-9799982-0-4

LIABILITY/WARRANTY:

The views and interpretations expressed in this book are the authors, and are not intended to provide exact or specific advice. The author shall not be liable for any loss or damage incurred in the process of following advice presented in this book.

All scripture quotations used have been taken from <u>The Holy Bible, New Living Translation</u> (NLT). Tyndale House Publishers Inc: Wheaton, Illinois, © 1996 and <u>The Good News Bible: The Bible in Today's English Version</u> (TEV), American Bible Society: New York, © 1976.

Special Prayer to the Reader

I dedicate my prayerful thoughts to every reader and to those who are near and dear to me. I support you and believe in you, as I am confident in your ability to achieve your goals and live a life of fulfillment. I pray that my words of compassion and kindness will uplift and encourage you through all the days of your life, and remind you that God is with you, every step of the way.

Table of Contents

Foreword 9
The Work God Does For You 15
   Accepting God's work 16
   Abandoning your doubt 20
   Lightening your heart with God's grace 27
   Bringing your heart home to God 30
   Delving Deep 33

The Energy God Gives You 41
   Hoping beyond hopelessness 42
   Moving past your discontent 49
   Letting God's power lighten your load 53
   Delving Deep 57

The Trust God Allows You 61
   Trusting in God 62
   Releasing your worries 64
   Removing your guilt 69
   Delving Deep 71

The Love God Feels For You 77
   Eliminating your arrogance 78
   Detaching your loneliness 81
   Gaining strength from grief 84
   Recognizing that God's love is forever 87
   Delving Deep 87

Powerful Affirmation 93
   With God I can do everything 93
   Delving Deep 102
   Afterward 105
   About the Author 110
   Volume Book Discounts 112

Acknowledgement and Dedication

Father in Heaven, in the Name of Jesus, have Your Way with this book.

Thank you God for all of your Blessings. Thank you God for your grace and mercy and favor.

Special thanks to everyone who has been and will be a blessing in my life.

My gratitude to the many people who invested in the development of this book project.

I would like to thank my parents Robert Sr. and Emma and my brother William for their constant and unconditional love and support.

----- Robert Moment

Foreword

When your best friend is God, you're never alone. There is great comfort in knowing that God will never leave you nor forsake you. God is with you in every situation, in every place.

Trust in God and anticipate the good that each day holds for you. Always be ready to experience the power of God in your life.

Be prepared for both the expected and unexpected blessings and rely on God as your compass. Life is about change, exploring, learning, and growth.

The world can seem senseless and chaotic but the power of God protects us and the presence of God watches over us.

Have you ever felt tired of living? Have you ever stopped to ask yourself what all of this is for? Have you ever wondered if your life has a purpose and a destiny? If you have, you're not alone.

Take a walk down a crowded street and look at the people all around you, knowing each and every person you see has asked themselves these very same questions. How many times? Once, twice, three times, who knows?

Have you ever had a bad day? Have you ever thought to yourself, "can my day get any worse"? Have you ever felt the world is a gloomy place full of miserable people who are out to get you and bring you down? If you have, you're not alone.

Everyone's had a bad day, and many people don't just have bad days, they have bad weeks, bad months and bad years. Look out a window into a busy street and watch the people that pass by. How many of them are suffering from being fired or laid off from their job, how many of them have just lost a loved one, how many of them are suffering from a terminal diseases, how many of them have no one to go home to, and how many more have no home at all? Is there anyone who cares?

Have you ever been disappointed in yourself? Have you ever thought if only you had done this better, you could have avoided that from happening? Have you ever felt so guilty that you wished you'd never been born? If you have, you're not alone.

Right now there are millions of people around the world who feel trapped, are tired of living with themselves, are wishing they had someone else's life, or wish they could have a fresh start at living. How many of the people that you encountered today do you think are filled with self regret and self hate? We've all become accustomed to hiding our true feelings so well, who can tell?

There is only one answer for the questions -

    Who knows?

    Who cares?

    Who can tell?

And the answer is God.

God knows that your life has purpose; through God you will gain stamina to want to live. God cares deeply for you and is always there to support you no matter what troubles face you; through God you will learn to care for yourself and for others. God can tell when you feel self-guilt and loathing; through God you will gain the courage to forgive yourself and accept yourself for who you are.

There are so many feelings we experience, so many choices, both good and bad that we must live with, and through it all, God is with us every step of the way. That is why *God Will Always Be There For You* has been created, to show you that there is someone who knows you better than you know yourself, someone who cares for you more than is humanly possible, and someone who can tell exactly what you are feeling and accept you for who you are without question.

In this book for the heart and soul you will discover how letting God into your life can help you overcome and accomplish anything, allowing you to live with purpose, grow in love, and cherish all the beauty that surrounds you. *God Will Always Be There For You* is about finding faith in God and making Him a part of your life. Faith is about believing and trusting in God, and when you have faith in God, you'll have faith in yourself.

The Work God Does For You

God is ever loving and ever forgiving. Through the power of His love we can learn many things and become better people. Trusting in God's work can help us become the best person we can be, allowing us to live a life that is fulfilling and full of love.

In order to allow God's grace to work, we need to let Him in by accepting His work, abandoning our doubt, lightening our heart and bringing our heart home to rest in God's house. We will find that everything can be achieved through faith.

"Listen to the words of the wise; apply your heart to my instruction." (Proverbs 22:17 NLT).

Accepting God's work

Accepting God's work is to turn away from the path of sin. The path of sin leads to a world that has no God in it, and every one of us has been tempted to follow this road. No one wants to think of themselves as a sinner, but sometimes we lose our way, and choose to put our wants before God's.

A world full of sin is a world in chaos. In order to co-exist in harmony, humans need to love and care for one another in the way God intended. Humanity can only implode in a world where everyone in it doesn't care about the needs of others, and is only concerned about getting what they want.

A mind that is corrupted with sin neither respects nor takes God seriously. God and His counsel are constantly rejected, leaving room only for sin.

Every sin, regardless of what it is, has one thing in common – the "I" factor. What is the "I" factor? It is when a person places his or her wants over the needs of others, or takes advantage of others to gain what they desire.

Committing sins doesn't only affect us; it also affects others and leads to chaos. We've all seen the chaos these sins can create. Parents ignore their children; children rebel against their parents. The husband takes his wife for granted; the wife lies to her husband. The old beguile the young; the young take advantage of the old. The tyrant murders the millions; the suppressed millions seek revenge on the tyrant. The chaos sin creates goes on and on, because one sin perpetuates another.

Our passions and emotions can sometimes make it easy for us to be misled by sin. That being said, there is no excuse for committing a sin.

In this life we have two choices:

1. Choose to follow God and warm our hearts by spreading His love.

2. Choose to follow sin and harden our hearts by spreading our despair.

In other words, it is the difference between choosing:

- Forgiveness and seeking revenge
- Loving and hating
- Satisfaction and greed
- Self-control and self-indulgence

At times it may seem easier to follow our own selfish actions and be tempted by the pressures of society, but in the end we only hurt ourselves, those we care about, and the one who loves us most – God.

Those who choose to accept God's work are happy and "do not follow the example of sinners or join those who have no use for God. Instead, they find joy in obeying the Law of the Lord, and...They succeed in everything they do." (Psalm 1:1-3 TEV)

Our constant worries and regrets often make it difficult for us to feel we are worthy of forgiveness and the more we sin, the more we worry and fall astray.

Just because we sin doesn't mean we won't be forgiven. God is forgiving; we are His children and He loves us. Thus, although we may occasionally sin, by accepting God's work we welcome Him into our hearts so sin can never claim us.

How do we accept God's work? The answer is plain and simple – believe in Him. Our faith will permit God to work in us, allowing Him to make His home in our hearts.

Abandoning your doubt

In our world it's easy to doubt the existence of God. Everyday we are subjected to sin and suffering. All we have to do is turn on the news or pick up the local newspaper and we'll likely find a natural disaster that claimed the life of thousands, a murder story, or some other deplorable event plastered all over the front page. With so much despair this often leads us to wonder "If God loves us so much, how can He sit back and watch his children suffer?"

The truth is, God doesn't sit back. Instead He follows each and every one of us, waiting for us to cast off our doubt, turn around and welcome Him with open arms.

We will abandon our doubt when we stop running away from God. God follows us wherever we go. He has been following you before the day you were born, and will do so until the day we die when He welcomes us into His home forever.

When we doubt God, we turn our backs on Him, leaving our minds to wonder. The more we wonder, the more our hearts fall into a spiritual wasteland. A spiritual wasteland is where we spend our time when we doubt God. It is a place where we second-guess our faith and question our beliefs.

As soon as we question our belief in God, we become confused and are tormented with doubt. Our thoughts begin to cling to the mundane and we fall back to basing most of our beliefs on things we can physically see, because we've grown up on the phrase: "I'll believe it when I see it".

Do the rules of science really show any physical evidence that God truly exists? We can't see Him, we can't hear Him speak, but by now we should know that religion does not follow the rules of science. Seeing isn't always believing.

Remember the story of one of the Lord's disciples, Thomas? He would not believe his fellow disciples that the Lord was raised from the dead and said, "Unless I see the scars of the nails in his hand and put my finger on those scars and my hand in his side, I will not believe." (John 20:25 TEV).

When the Lord appeared before Thomas, He let Thomas touch his scars, and upon seeing them, Thomas instantly believed. Christ then said to

Thomas: "Do you believe because you see me? How happy are those who believe without seeing me!" (John 20:29 TEV)

It's only human for us sometimes to doubt like Thomas, but you would be surprised to learn the many ways God reveals Himself to us when we aren't even paying attention. For instance: Have you ever received kindness from a total stranger? Have you ever been captivated by a beautiful sunset? Have you ever felt love for someone and had that love returned? Have you ever seen a smile brighten up a child's face? If you've experienced any of these wonders, have you not sensed the presence of God?

When we sense God through beautiful wonders in our life, we need to let go of our uncertainty and give our doubts to Him. Although we may find it hard to let go at first, with time it will become easier.

To help us abandon our doubt we can follow these simple steps:

- **Live outside the moment** – It is easy for us to become wrapped up in our daily lives and live in each moment, feeling as if it will last for an eternity. For instance, when we become ill, sometimes we can think of nothing past the misery of pain and suffering. But when we embrace God, we can live outside our physical moments and know that regardless of what we may go through, we have an almighty Father who will be with us all the days of our lives.

- **Evaluate your worth through God's eyes** – At certain times in our lives when we are feeling really low and confused, we may feel that we are unworthy of love and kindness. The next time you feel downtrodden, remember that God loves you and He is with you always; in good times and in bad. We are worthy of God's love. If we weren't, He wouldn't make the effort to follow us.

- **Trust your Faith** – Faith is stronger than feelings. It's only natural that we won't feel connected to God every day, but the way we feel has no effect on the presence of God in our lives. Although there will be days when we won't feel the presence of God, we need to remember on these days the trust we have in our faith. It is through our faith that the grace and goodness of God will follow us wherever our life may lead us. Regardless of how we may feel, when we have our faith, God's mercy is with us every step of the way.

Having faith is about trust. If we put our trust in God we will abandon our doubt. Should our faith ever falter, we need to remember the words spoken in Psalm 23: "I know that your goodness and love will be with me all my life; and your house will be my home as long as I live." (Psalm 23:6 TEV).

When we abandon our doubt, we will find that God has been and always will be with us.

Lightening your heart with God's grace

In our society we have the tendency to put labels on people and in turn have labels placed upon ourselves. Every day we battle stereotypes and criticism while we try to meet the standards that have been placed before us. Often we end up defining ourselves based on the ideals of society.

What ideals does society care about? It cares about our…

- Salary
- Appearance
- Attitude
- Integrity
- Personality
- Intelligence
- Etc.

According to society, each of these physical and mental attributes defines us as a person. Sometimes, when we are judged by our characteristics, the result is negative. People see us as lazy, old fashioned, a quitter, unreliable, boring and slow to learn. Other times, we are judged in a positive light and may be considered successful, attractive, dynamic, conscientious, intriguing and clever.

Whether the results are negative or positive, we tend to believe what others think of us, and in some cases, will go out of our way to try and please a society that in truth, knows very little about the people we actually are.

Thus, while we, our family, friends and co-workers may define us through these ideals, God doesn't care about these trivial attributes and instead defines us through grace, not criticism.

What are the ideals grace upholds?

- Spirituality
- Union with God
- Faith
- Love

Through God's grace each and every one of us is seen as a unique and brilliant work of art. He takes all the aspects of our life and molds them together into a sculpture of His love.

By letting the grace of God enter our hearts and souls, it will slowly begin to define us. The more grace seeps into our being, the more it will purge society's labels from us. Eventually we will discover that grace is what grants us mercy, not the deeds we do in this life.

The grace of God will fill us when we abandon our doubt, embrace our faith, and accept God's work. Always remember, regardless of what anyone may say, you are not who they think you are, you are who God thinks you are: "By God's grace I am what I am." (1 Corinthians 15:10 TEV).

Bringing your heart home to God

Until we reach the home of our Heavenly Father we are all orphans on this earth, waiting until the day when we can join God forever. Even though we are orphans, we can still be close to God by letting Him make His home in our heart while we are bound to this Earth.

How can we make a home for God in our hearts, so one day we can bring our hearts home to God?

First and foremost we need to turn away from sin and choose to accept His work. Accepting God's work is to recognize that He has provided us with a beautiful gift. God sacrificed His only son to free us from the burden of sin. Christ, who had never sinned, "died for sins once and for all…in order to lead you to God." (1 Peter 3:18 TEV).

Second, we need to trust our faith. Believing in God is the ultimate level of trust, because our belief cannot be strengthened through physical evidence. It can only grow stronger through spirituality and obedience to God. Thus, having faith is knowing that "What can be seen lasts only for a time, but what cannot be seen lasts forever." (2 Corinthians 4:18 TEV)

Third, we need to live in the company of God's grace. It's no secret that most of us want to know what we need to do in order to get into Heaven. Just as the jailer asked in Acts 16:30, "what must I do to be saved?" The answer was then, and still remains, "Believe in the Lord Jesus, and you will be saved." (Acts 16:31 TEV). Believing means having faith and trust in God completely. With God's grace, mercy shall follow us like an invisible cloud that will one day carry us to Heaven.

Finally, in order to bring our hearts home to God, we need to be at peace with ourselves and learn to let go of our fear of death. It is only our physical bodies that die with our sins. Without our bodies our orphaned souls are released, allowing us to find our way back home to our Father. When we are ready to accept the death of our earthly body, we will gain a newfound courage and discover "We…would much prefer to leave our home in the body and be at home with the Lord." (2 Corinthians 5:8 TEV).

Bringing our heart home to God is the ultimate goal of faith. It is where our heart longs to be. God's home is a nurturing paradise that keeps us safe from all evil, frees us from suffering and wraps us in a warm blanket of utter happiness. In God's home, we are recognized as His children, and to express His joy for our return, He gives us His everlasting love and life.

Delving Deep

After reading the above section "**The Work God Does For You**," you may find that certain feelings or memories have resurfaced. Before you continue on to the next section, take a moment to stop and think on the following questions that correspond to the first segment of the book.

Note: If you wish, you can record your answers directly in the space provided in this book, or you can write your answers on a piece of paper, a pad or in a special journal.

Accepting God's Work

1. Have you ever felt satisfaction from giving in to temptations? Explain.

2. Do you find the power of temptation demanding? If so, in what ways do you find it demanding?

3. Have there ever been times in your life when you lost faith in God? What were the reasons for your actions? Did you feel justified? Why?

Abandoning your Doubt

1. Do you have a hard time believing God exists? If so, why do you feel this way?

2. Do you frequently rely on your feelings? Have your feelings ever let you down, or overwhelmed you so much that you have felt as if you would be stuck in a single hopeless moment for eternity? If so, describe these moments and explain why you lost all hope for the future?

3. Do you believe that you can become closer to God? In what ways do you think you can become closer to God?

4. What keeps you from expressing your faith in God?

Lightening your Heart with God's Grace

1. Do you care what society thinks of you, and do you try to meet its demands or the demands of others?

2. Have you ever done good acts with the hope that they will qualify you for Heaven? If so, what made you feel compelled to do so?

3. Do you believe God's goodness is blessing you? If so, do you meet each day knowing that unlimited good is before you and that it may show up in the most unexpected ways?

BRINGING YOUR HEART HOME TO GOD

1. Are you afraid of death? If so, what do you think would help ease your fears?

2. If you considered Heaven your real home, would this make a difference to how you currently live your life? Would it make a difference to your fear of death?

3. Everyone dreams of Heaven. What does Heaven look like to you?

The Energy God Gives You

When we accept God into our lives, we receive a new- found energy and confidence that will get us through anything. Therefore, regardless of what happens in our life, no amount of anguish we may feel can ever diminish our hope. This means the energy God gives us is hope, and this hope is born from our faith. Trust that nothing will happen to you without God's permission and He will give you strength to endure.

As we face and overcome difficult times in our lives, the energy God gives us will increase and our desire to bring our heart home to Him will grow stronger. In this section we'll explore how

God's energy can help us embrace spirituality so we can move victoriously past times of suffering.

Hoping beyond hopelessness

We've all hoped and we've all dreamed, but there have also been times when we've despaired. Times of despair are not easy, especially when we are trapped in a helpless situation, comforts from humans cannot soothe our pain and we have abandoned all hope.

It is difficult to hold on to hope when we see suffering all around us; when we lose faith in ourselves; when we become ill; or we lose someone we love. But we will always have hope if we believe that God's wisdom, knowledge and power surpasses ours, therefore He is in control of the situation even if you might not think so, because you are looking at the situation with the physical eye.

Some of us have felt hopelessness because of heartbreaking experiences such as:

- **Natural disasters**: Losing our home, friends or loved ones to a natural disaster such as a hurricane, earthquake, tornado or fire, is devastating. All around us is suffering and everything we once knew and held dear has been destroyed. Essentially, we need to hope for the better, pick up the pieces and start a whole new life, placing your hope in God to provide again for you as He did before. Place your concerns before the maker of the universe and ask Him to intervene.

  Is hoping another disaster won't come our way the answer to eliminating our despair? No. The hope that God will always be with us and protect us no matter what comes our way is how we will stop the cycle of hopelessness. It is how you react and deal with disaster that needs to change. *"God is our shelter and our strength, always ready to help in times of trouble. So we will not be afraid, even if the earth is shaken and mountains fall into the ocean depths;" (Psalm 46:1-2 TEV).*

- **Loss of a loved one**: No words can describe the absolute anguish of losing someone we love. When someone close to us dies, we carry a scar on our hearts for the rest of our life, because that person had become a part of who we are, and is now gone from our Earthy lives forever.

When we put our loved ones to rest, we feel as if we are burying our hope along with them. Many times we plummet into a state of hopelessness because we blame God for taking that someone we loved away too soon.

It takes time, but our hope will be restored when we understand that it was God's plan to welcome our loved one into His home forever. Their death was not meant to make us suffer; it was to end their suffering. We will overcome our hopelessness when we don't hold our hurts against God, forgive ourselves, and ask God's help to move forward.

Our hope will be restored when we remember that we will again see the ones we love when our soul is welcomed home to God. Physically dying is not the worse thing that can happen to your loved one. The state of their heart with God is what matters the most therefore it is our duty to help loved ones give their hearts to God while they are still alive. *"Turn to me, Lord, and be merciful to me, because I am lonely and weak. Relieve me of my worries and save me from all my troubles. Consider my distress and suffering and forgive all my sins." (Psalm 25:16-18 TEV).*

- **Illness**: The world is full of many deadly diseases and the last thing anyone wants is to suffer through a disease such as cancer. Unfortunately, when it comes to physical illness, there isn't much we can do to prevent it from happening if we become a chosen target of illness and disease. God has given us the same power that raised Jesus from the dead to cast out all spirits of illnesses.

Going through an illness is anything but easy. It puts a strain on our body and our mind. We become weary with pain, and the thought of dying or future suffering is both stressful and depressing. This is the work of the enemy to steal your joy, health and time by creating doubt in you about God's existence.

Furthermore, when we are ill we often feel alone, even if we have plenty of support from our friends and family. Part of the reason why we feel alone is because we don't believe the people who are supporting us understand what we are going through. When we add all these aspects together, it's easy to lose hope and fall into despair.

When you believe you have God by your side, all hope is not lost. God will never leave you, and He will continue to hold your hand and give you comfort, regardless if you overcome your illness or come to rest in Heaven. *"Even if I go through the deepest darkness, I will not be afraid, Lord, for you are with me." (Psalm 23:4 TEV)*

- **Failure**: Nobody likes to fail at anything they do. Receiving our first "F" on an exam or a term paper is a serious shock to our system, especially when we are not expecting it. It's the same shock that occurs when we are fired or laid off from a job, or even when we file for a divorce or end any type of relationship.

Failure can make us doubt ourselves, which makes us lose faith in our abilities. When we lose faith in ourselves, we can lose hope in achieving our future goals. However, even though we may not be able to express our insecurities to others, God already knows the person we are and still continues to believe in us, just as we believe in Him. He will provide us with the support we need, to help us get back on our feet and prepare us for a better tomorrow. *"I am surrounded by many troubles – too many to count…I am weak and poor, O Lord, but you have not forgotten me." (Psalm 40:12…17 TEV).*

We do not know where the roads of this life will lead us. One day while we may be successful in our job, the next we could be jobless. We may be healthy today, only to find out tomorrow that we have a terminal illness. We don't know what life has in store for us, and we can't change the plan God has designed for us. What we can do, however, is strive to lead a good life, and live our lives in the best way we've been shown how in God's word and believe that God is at our side.

Moving past your discontent

When you were a child, you likely had plenty of hopes and dreams. When someone asked you what you wanted to be when you grew up, you probably had an answer, as well as every intention of making your dream a reality. Things were simpler when you were young. You knew what you liked, what you wanted, and for the most part, you were content with what you had.

However, as time passes and as we become adults, our lives change, and so does our view of the world. Instead of following a simple path, we tend to bite off more than we can chew. We succumb to greed and compare ourselves with others. This is partially due to the fact that we live in an extremely materialistic society that is constantly telling us that in order to live more fulfilling lives we need to buy things.

We have grown accustomed to wanting things we don't need. We fool ourselves into believing we need frivolous items that won't make us any more satisfied than what we already have. All we do is accumulate more and more junk; temporal things which in turn cause us more and more discontent: "Human desires are like the world of the dead – there is always room for more." (Proverbs 27:20 TEV)

We will stop feeling discontent when we learn to be happy with ourselves and stop pursuing things we don't need. Happiness is an inside job. It starts with self-love. Develop a strong love for yourself and know that God made you in His own image. There is no one like you. There never has been never will be. Say out loud, "I Accept and Love Myself" and "I am a Child of God" and "God Loves Me Unconditionally".

You are God's Precious Gift that's uniquely, wonderfully and marvelously made. Think about it, what provides us with more fulfillment; loving yourself and receiving love in return, or buying the latest sports car on the market? How about spending quality time with our loved ones, or being a workaholic so we can afford the costs of our expensive tastes?

Our discontent grows as our bank accounts deplete. The less we can buy, the more distraught we become and the less satisfied we feel with our lives. Without question, our reasons for feeling discontent are foolish. We are in a constant state of unhappiness because we can't think outside the box of materialism.

We have money and we are unhappy because we want more. We go into debt and we are unhappy because we don't have enough money. And this never-ending circle of greed will continue until you stop running around in it and face just God.

When we trust and accept God's will in our lives, we can pass our burden of discontent on to Him, and lighten our lot in life by following the example He sets: "Show me the path where I should walk, O Lord; point out the right road for me to follow" (Psalm 25:4 NLT)

Aside from the basic necessities of food, water and a roof over your head, there are really only two things we need in this life that will bring us fulfillment and make us truly happy. Total fulfillment in life is knowing and loving God.

Letting God's power lighten your load

Have you ever been on a vacation and had to drag all your luggage through the airport, or do you remember how heavy your backpack was when it was loaded down with school books? How relieved were you when you could set down all your baggage and relax? It likely felt as though a weight had been lifted from your shoulders. That is exactly what having God in your life can do for you – lighten your load. Let God drive and you can relax and enjoy the ride.

We carry around a lot of unnecessary baggage everyday, all the time. Not real physical baggage, but the mental baggage of burden. Sure, it sounds silly that mental baggage can tire us out, but carrying around our burdens all the time is just as tiring as carrying a complete set of luggage full of bricks.

What type of burdens do we carry?

- Worry
- Guilt
- Grief
- Loneliness
- Fear
- Weariness
- Discontent
- Doubt

Why do we carry these burdens? For many of us it is because we've been carrying them around for most of our lives and have become accustomed to doing so. It always seems that when we let one burden go, it is replaced by three or four more. To make matters worse, we don't just carry around our burdens, but also the burdens of others.

With all these burdens we carry, no wonder we are ready to drop from exhaustion at the end of the day and we can't sleep at night. That being said, it doesn't have to be this way. God is offering His arms to help us carry our load. All we need to do is let Him teach us how to learn to let go of the things we cannot change and accept His help: "I am worn out, O Lord; have pity on me! Give me strength; I am completely exhausted." (Psalm 6:2 TEV).

Think about it, if you have a child, would you let your son or daughter drag a large suitcase around the airport? Of course you wouldn't. You would take the large luggage from your children, because they can not handle such a burden.

This is how God feels toward us. We are His children, and He knows we are carrying far too much baggage than we can, or were ever meant to bear. God wants to help carry our burden, perhaps it's time we shared or lessened our load.

Delving Deep

After reading the above section "**The Energy God Gives You**," you may find that certain feelings or memories have resurfaced. Before you continue on to the next section, take a moment to stop and think on the following questions that correspond to the first segment of the book.

Note: If you wish, you can record your answers directly in the space provided in this book, or you can write your answers on a piece of paper, a pad or in a special journal.

HOPING BEYOND HOPELESSNESS

1. When was the last time you felt hopeless? Why did you feel this way?

2. Do you think accepting God's work is all the hope you'll ever need? Explain

3. When you are in despair do you tend to push away the ones who love you the most? If so, why do you reject their help?

Moving past your discontent

1. Do you remember the dreams you had in your youth? Were you able to achieve all your dreams, or did you give up on them? Do you think achieving a personal goal will help you feel content?

2. Are you a slave to materialism? Do you often want what you can't have, or don't need?

3. In your opinion, what is the difference between having what you want and wanting what you have? Does obtaining what you want make your life any more satisfying than that which you already have? Explain

Letting God's Power Lighten Your Load

1. What are your primary or most pressing burdens (pertaining to your relationships, friends, spouse, career, finances, etc.)?

2. Why do you carry these burdens with you? Do you feel you deserve them? What steps will you take to overcome your burdens?

3. Are you willing to let go of all of your burdens, turn to God and let Him take the load? Do you have confidence in Him to keep His word?

The Trust God Allows You

If there is anyone we can trust in our lives, it's God. God is the only aspect of our life that will remain inclusive and constant. His love for us never changes, nor does His goal of following us through our life, so He can one day take us to His home forever.

Trusting in God is extremely important if we ever want our faith to change our life for the better. When we trust or believe God's love for us, the more comfortable we will become with the person we are, and the more apt we will be to release unnecessary burdens such as worry and grief, so we can follow the path and the plans He has already prepared for us.

Trusting in God

Have you ever had complete trust in someone? For instance, if you went to visit your doctor for your annual checkup, and he or she informed you that you were in good health but your cholesterol was a little high, would you second- guess your doctor's advice about lowering your salt intake, or trust his or her council?

If you're like most people, you'll likely trust your doctor's advice. After all, he or she has a degree in medicine, licensed by an approving authority, and that should count for something. Even doctors try to find the "origin" of something about you in order to solve your issues- family history. The same can be said for God. Remember, by God's spirit you were created. He is your origin and your history. You're not just made up of body but of soul that doctors cannot touch or help. God is the final Judge in saving souls, in fact, He created the whole universe, so there isn't anyone better we can turn to if we're looking for someone who knows our body and soul .

Want another reason why we can put our trust in God? God has no hidden agenda; all His cards are on the table. God's one true goal is to follow us through our earthly life and protect our soul from evil. God is our guardian. All He wants is our safety, so He will do all that. He can protect our orphaned soul to ensure that one day we reach home safe and sound.

If we cannot trust God, we can trust no one: "acknowledge that I alone am God and that there is no one else like me. From the beginning I predicted the outcome; long ago I foretold what would happen. I said that my plans would never fail, that I would do everything I intended to do." (Isaiah 46:9-10 TEV).

We must let our fears go, abandon all our doubts, and embrace God for who He is.

Releasing your worries

One of the biggest burdens many of us tend to drag around is worry. We worry about everything. We worry about:

- Yesterday, today and tomorrow
- Meeting the expectations of others
- Being a good parent
- Being a good spouse/partner
- Careers
- Money
- Making the right decisions
- Failure

- Death
- And the list can go on and on

All of which you don't have control over. Worrying cannot add a single thing to a situation – it doesn't change anything for good. When we worry, we're not only preoccupied with the pressures of today's priorities, but we're also concerned about future possibilities. Thus, instead of focusing our mind on things that really matter, we're preoccupied with things we don't know will happen, and that we can't change if they do happen.

This is why worrying is ridiculous. Why? Because worrying has no positive impact on the outcome of what we're worrying about. To put it plain and simple: if we worry about something and it doesn't come to pass, then our worry was wasted, and if we worry about something that does come to pass, our worry was pointless.

Aside from the fact that worry does not affect an outcome positively, it can affect other things such as our physical and mental health. Too much worry in our life can be an attributing factor to real illnesses such as heart trouble, high blood pressure, migraine headaches, blindness, malfunctions of the thyroid and various stomach disorders such as ulcers. Furthermore, worrying can lower our self esteem and cause us to become paranoid and insecure.

God does not want us to worry or fear. God did not give us a spirit of worry, fear, or doubt. Although we don't know where our life is headed, God does, and He drives and He holds the map. All He wants us to do is to accept His love for us and follow the path He has laid before us, so we can be the best we can be.

Here are examples of some of the more common worries we are faced with, and how these worries can be overcome if we trust in God's wisdom and complete knowledge of us and our issues:

- **Money** – "Confidence placed in riches comes to nothing." (Proverbs 11:7 TEV)

- **Work** - "Work hard and do not be lazy. Serve the Lord with a heart full of devotion." (Romans 12:11 TEV)

- **Personal Character** – "O Lord, you have examined my heart and know everything about me." (Psalm 139:1 NLT).

- **Facing life alone** – "So the person who marries does well, and the person who doesn't marry does even better." (1 Corinthians 7:38 NLT)

While we do feel obligation to meet the demands of some of our worries, we need to take a look at the bigger picture and trust in God. We cannot change the path God has created for us, so there's no sense in worrying about it. After all, God follows us every step of the way, so we don't ever have to worry about Him abandoning us. Ask Him to give you the power to resist the many temptations on the sides of the path that are trying to keep you off course.

Let your worries go every second, every minute, and daily. Make a decision not to savor worries in your mind when they appear. Choose "faith," not fear.

Removing your guilt

There are times when we all feel guilt. We feel guilt about what we should have done and what we didn't do. Just guilt by itself is not good for you. When you feel guilt and your conscience tells you your actions are – or were- wrong, you feel remorse and regret in your heart. Ask God for forgiveness and believe that He has granted it. If not properly handled, guilt can slow you down and become more deadly than the act that caused it. Guilt can make us second guess ourselves, can cause worry, and make us feel obligated to do things for the wrong reasons. We try to undo what we did and even accept the guilt as a deserved punishment for what we did.

We cannot forget our regrets, but we need to let our regrets go. Holding on to regrets is not healthy, because we cannot live our life on what-ifs. We cannot change what has come to pass no matter how hard we try. We must accept our mistakes and move on with our lives, regrets can only hold us back from living in the present; and it is the present that deserves our undivided attention.

Apart from holding on to regrets, guilt also pressures us into doing things for the wrong reasons. For instance, if we feel guilt for wronging someone, we may want to make things right with the person only because we feel guilty and not because we want to.

When we feel guilty, we are unhappy and disappointed with ourselves, and we may feel undeserving of compassion. However, the truth is, we are not alone. Everyone has felt guilty at least once in their life time, because, "no one does what is right, not even one." (Romans 3:12 TEV)

God knows everything about us. He is both omnipotent and omniscient and understands us implicitly. God knows us better than we know ourselves. We do not need to hide from God. He knows when we make mistakes and He knows when we are truly remorseful about something.

We are not without sin, and God knows and loves us anyway.

Trust in God and let your guilt go. We have nothing to be ashamed of if we remain true to our faith in God.

Delving Deep

After reading the above section "**The Trust God Allows You**," you may find certain feelings or memories have resurfaced. Before you continue on to the next section, take a moment to stop and think about the following questions that correspond to the first segment of the book.

Note: If you wish, you may record your answers directly in the space provided in this book, or write your answers on a piece of paper, a pad or in a special journal.

Trusting in God

1. Have you ever had any reason not to put your full trust in God? If so, explain.

2. What does trust mean to you?

3. Does knowing you can put your trust in God give you more confidence in God and make your faith stronger?

Releasing your worries

1. What do you worry about and why?

2. Have you ever made yourself physically sick or become mentally exhausted from your worry?

3. Do you believe that trusting in God's work releases your worries?

4. What is the greatest internal pressure you feel in your life?

5. What is the greatest external pressure you feel in your life?

Removing your guilt

1. Do you carry around guilt with you? What do you feel guilty about? Do you want God to help you change this?

2. Do you sometimes feel guilty for things that aren't your fault? Why do you suppose you feel this way?

3. Do you think holding on to guilt makes you a better person? Or do you think your guilt holds you back from being the best person you can be? Explain

The Love God Feels For You

The love God feels for us is unconditional and whole. He does not love us so that we will follow or choose Him; He loved us before there was a reason because we need Him more than He needs us.

Through the love God feels for us, we will not only be able to overcome arrogance, loneliness and grief, but also become a better friend, parent, child, and spouse (partner) - and most importantly - a better follower of God.

The love God feels for us is something that is truly special and irreplaceable. And if we let it, God's love will transform us into compassionate beings that show His love for us through our love for one another: "if we love one another, God lives in union with us, and his love is made perfect in us." (1 John 4:12 TEV)

ELIMINATING YOUR ARROGANCE

Being proud in gratitude of who we are, and proud of others around us, is a good thing. Good pride keeps us motivated and helps us believe in ourselves and others. But having too much pride is bad and can make us arrogant.

When we become arrogant, we become selfish, foolish, petty and insensitive. We forget to consider the feelings of others and we lose sight of what is truly important – compassion.

Without compassion we can not truly relate to others or eat a slice of humble pie. Arrogance causes us to listen with closed ears and twists reality to our favor so we only hear what we want to. We're quicker to speak than listen. Arrogance misleads us into believing we are wise and do not need the opinions of others.

It is human folly to let arrogance get the better of our lives, because we should never consider ourselves better than anyone else: "Do not be proud, but accept humble duties. Do not think of yourselves as wise." (Romans 12:16 TEV). We're like hand-painted eggs- we come in a variety of colors and designs but inside we're all eggs. Humans are the same everywhere in the world and only differ by skin tone.

Arrogance disappoints God and breaks His heart. He loves all His children equally and does not want to see them fighting among themselves, or thinking that one is better than the other. There is no harm in feeling proud to be loved by God, but His love should not make us feel that we are better than anyone else. What's unique about us should make us proud of our God and Father for His wisdom and design. He's the great artist and we're His masterpieces.

Eliminating your arrogance makes us better people because it allows us to think with a clear mind and an open heart. Without arrogance we will become better people who draw respect and compassion from others, because "good people will be generous to others and will be blessed for all they do." (Isaiah 32:8 NLT).

God loves us for who we are, He does not love our arrogance when we pretend to be in control or something we're not. Of course, there will be times when our pride may get the better of us, but always remember - it's never too late to say you're sorry.

Detaching your loneliness

All of us want to feel loved and protected. We've wanted this since the day we were born and will continue to want it until the day we die. Feeling loved and protected provides us with courage and contentment, makes us feel safe – and above all – not feel alone.

When we feel alone, we become scared, lost, rejected and filled with despair. We give up all hope and often turn to self-pity for comfort, which turns out to be a poor substitute for human compassion or companionship.

Some of the many reasons why we may feel loneliness include:

- Rejection from friends, parents or spouse/partner
- Abuse (verbal and physical)

- Divorce
- Death of a loved one
- Living with someone who pays you no attention and shows you no kindness

Depending on the depth of loneliness we feel, it may be next to impossible to overcome our loneliness on our own. But that's all right; we needn't despair or worry about doing anything on our own, because God is always with us.

With God by our side He will…

- **Eliminate your fear** - "There is no fear in love; perfect love drives out all fear." (1 John 4:18 TEV)

- **Rescue you from abandonment** - "Even if my father and mother abandon me the Lord will hold me close." (Psalm 27:10 NLT).

- **Give you courage** - "You, O Lord, are always my shield from danger; you give me victory and restore my courage." (Psalm 3:3 TEV)

- **Provide Protection** -"He provides help and protection for righteous, honest people. He protects those who treat others fairly, and guards those who are devoted to him." (Proverbs 2:7-8 TEV).

You may not be able to see God, but if you trust your faith and believe in Him and in His purpose for your life, you will feel His presence in your life. You will know He loves you and you will know that no matter what trials you may face, you are never alone: "The Lord is my Shepherd; I have everything I need." (Psalm 23:1 NLT).

GAINING STRENGTH FROM GRIEF

The pain and suffering caused by grief is something we never quite get over. Usually this is because we have suffered the loss of a loved one. Grief can often make us feel alone, miserable and depressed. It can make us reject the kindness of others, and throw us into the depths of despair.

However, grief can also cause us to feel anger and resentment towards …

- **Ourselves** –You may feel guilt and regret for the death of a loved one, and think that maybe you could have done something, or said something that would have made a difference.

- **Others** –You feel that other people don't understand your pain, so you push them away and isolate yourself from everyone.

- **The deceased** –You are angry that they left you.
- **God** –You blame God for letting the one you love die.

In our state of grief, we often fail to realize that while we are grieving for a loss, we should also be rejoicing. Why? Because if we believe and trust in God, we know that death is only the beginning of a whole new life with God. A life that is free of pain, suffering and sin.

Therefore, when we grieve, never forget that God is standing beside us. When we weep, we are weeping on His shoulder. God loves us, and He will see us through anything.

Finally, remember that you are not the only one who feels grief. All around you are people who suffer from the loneliness, heartache and misery that grief causes. In times of grief, just as it is important to know that God is with us, it is also important to let others who are grieving know that we are there for them as well, because "A friend is always loyal, and a brother is born to help in time of need." (Proverbs 17:17 NLT).

We will gain strength from grief when we share our grief with others and we realize that those we grieve for are in a better place with God. A place we too will one day call our home.

Recognizing that God's love is forever

Realizing that God's love is forever is to know that God's love is all inclusive. His love for us will be the same tomorrow, as it was yesterday, and as it is today. Friends and family will come and go, but God's love remains forever.

How can God's love remain constant and forever you may wonder? It is because God's love outlasts death. Just as God is eternal, so is His love, because "God is love." (1 John 4:8 TEV). He is the beginning and the end of everything.

Delving Deep

After reading the above section, "**The Love God Feels For You**," you may find that certain feelings or memories have resurfaced. Before you continue on to the next section, take a moment to stop and think about the following questions that correspond to the first segment of the book.

Note: If you wish, you can record your answers directly in the space provided in this book, or write your answers on a piece of paper, a pad or in a special journal.

Eliminating your arrogance

1. Have you ever let your pride get the better of you? What was the outcome? Did you learn from it?

2. Do you think it is wrong to have pride in yourself? When do you think pride becomes too much?

3. Do you know someone who is arrogant? What types of characteristics does arrogance reveal about them?

Detaching Your Loneliness

1. Have you ever experienced loneliness? If so, did you overcome it? How? If not, do you fear loneliness?

2. Describe what loneliness means to you? If you find it hard putting it down in words, try making a sketch or a drawing to define your thoughts.

3. Does trusting in God and knowing that He is with you all the days of your life bring you comfort?

Gaining strength from grief

1. Is knowing that God is with you through your time of grief a great comfort to you? Explain.

2. When was the last time you helped someone in their time of grief? What did you say to comfort them?

3. Why do you think the greater our struggle in life, the greater the blessing?

Recognizing that God's love is forever

1. How would you define everlasting love?

2. Now that you know God's love is forever, does this change the way you feel about Him?

Powerful Affirmation

Having God in your life provides you with exceptional positive power. Suddenly everything you believed to be beyond your reach becomes an achievable goal. That's what powerful affirmation is all about, declaring that with God in your life you can do anything.

With God I can do everything

Do you ever feel intimidated by your goals and feel like you have too much on your plate to accomplish anything for yourself? If you have a family to look after, have bills to pay, or are trapped in an unrewarding job, you may feel as if you don't have time for yourself and are overwhelmed by stress.

These negative thoughts can crush our spirit and make any small obstacle in our lives appear or seem like a mountain. When we are feeling suffocated with the pressures of our daily lives, and we feel there is no one else we can turn to, this is an opportunity to turn to God.

God provides us with everything we need and more. We can depend on God to give us what we need in the right way and in the right time. He will hold our hand through the darkest of times and will never leave us no matter what happens. He judges us by the person we truly are.

If you need a positive spirit or energy boost in your life to get through daily and in times of struggle, or to help you entrust your goals, trust in powerful affirmation and…

- Before you start your day and before you go to bed say to yourself:
  "With God I can do everything"

- Before you eat your daily meals say to yourself:
  "With God I can do everything"

- When you're feeling down say to yourself:
  "With God I can do everything"

- When you're feeling happy say to yourself:
  "With God I can do everything"

God placed power in His word and with it all things were created. You have His spirit in you to speak His promise and make it happen.

The more we become accustomed to saying "with God I can do everything," the more we will believe its truth and realize it, and the more our faith will grow stronger.

When a powerful affirmation becomes an active part of your life, you can:

- Achieve both your personal and professional goals
- Become a great parent
- Become a great spouse or partner
- Become a great friend
- Find a rewarding job
- Live out your life's true purpose
- Get out of financial debt
- Become a successful entrepreneur
- Conquer an illness
- Have power over sin

The list can go on and on – our spiritual authority is limitless.

Never forget, we are invaluable to God and He wants to see us succeed. He knows our weakness and strengths. By following God's will we'll learn how we can use our strengths to become a leader and take charge of our life, so we can realize our goals and become a better person.

There is nothing like the power of faith and trust in God. It can make us achieve what we once thought was impossible and transform us into the best we can be. For instance, by making God's will an active part of your lifestyle, you gain:

Knowledge – There is more to knowledge than earning a college degree. When it comes to spiritual knowledge, true wisdom comes from understanding God's teachings and putting them into practice. We will not only learn to recognize sin and choose the path away from it, but we will also learn how to hear and listen.

Listening is how we become wise. One of the most important aspects in a relationship, regardless if it is a relationship between two friends, a parent and child, or life partners, is communication. Communication isn't just expressing your opinions and feelings, but is also about listening to the other person's opinions and feelings as well.

When you choose to follow the will of God and His plan, you walk in His guidance and gain wisdom through His will and plan for your life and His teachings of the word: "It is the Lord who gives wisdom; from him comes knowledge and understanding." (Proverbs 2:6 TEV)

Compassion - Sure, we've all felt sympathy for the homeless man or woman on the street, but when was the last time we acted on our feelings instead of just letting our empathy go to waste or passing out judgment? Don't miss the miracle of the moment to show compassion and be a blessing to others in need.

The more spiritual wisdom we obtain, the more we will be able to relate to others and understand that regardless of our ethnicity, gender, or age, we are all God's children and deserve His mercy and His love.   With compassion, we will gain a higher level of understanding and will be able to empathize with those who suffer without feeling they deserve their grief. We will also be able to celebrate the joy of someone else's happiness without feeling petty jealousy.   When we are compassionate we are not judgmental.

You will find that instead of just feeling compassion for others, you will begin to act on it and share in their grief or joy: "our love should not just be words and talk; it must be true love, which shows itself in action." (1 John 3:18 TEV).

Courage – It's only human to fear the unknown or to want to quit when the going gets tough. In a demanding society it doesn't take much for us to shy away from a challenge and want to choose the easier path. But with trust in God, we have the confidence to face new challenges, step out in faith and take the opportunities He has for us.

Remember, God is with you every step of the way. Therefore, should you feel that confidence is slipping from your grasp, you can have belief in God's total control and dominion over everything in your life and this world. He will guide you the rest of the way and you'll see it through together: "He renews my strength. He guides me along right paths, bringing honor to his name." (Psalm 23:3 NLT).

Whatever you may be facing or experiencing right now in your life, you can make it through – don't give up! It may be easy to quit, but your faith will pull you through. Nothing is impossible with God on your team.

Don't get discouraged. Have an attitude of expectation and maintain a positive mental outlook on this life. God wants us to be encouraged and not discouraged, so take the time to look back on your life so you can count all your joy and count your blessings.

When you believe in God, accept His work and let Him love you. Through His love you will see every day as a blessing, because every day you have on this Earth is a gift from God.

Continue to walk by faith and cast all your worries aside, because God's powerful affirmation lives inside you. All you need to do is tell yourself, "I can do everything with the help of Christ who gives me the strength I need." (Philippians 4:13 NLT).

Let Go and Let God lead.

Delving Deep

After reading the above section "**Affirmation**," you may find that certain feelings or goals have resurfaced. Before you continue on to the Afterward, take a moment to stop and think about the following questions that correspond to the first segment of the book.

Note: If you wish, you can record your answers directly in the space provided in this book, or write your answers on a piece of paper, a pad or in a special journal.

With God I can do everything

1. Is there something in your life you would like to achieve but have always felt was beyond your reach? What has stopped you from achieving your goals?

2. Do you believe having faith in God can help you achieve your goals? If so, explain. If not, explain.

3. What do you think will make your life more fulfilling?

Afterward

When your heart is weak and weary and your mind is overwhelmed with thoughts of regret, what-ifs and feelings of "how will I get through this," and you feel you don't have the strength to face another day, stop running and turn to God.

Complete faith in God is the best gift you can ever give to yourself. Faith is a hard teacher. Faith gives us the test before we get the lesson. Faith is the greatest asset you have as a believer in Jesus Christ. God wants your faith to be developed. Regardless of your past and present situations God honors faith. Without faith it is impossible to please God. Faith will work for you. "What is Faith? It is the confident assurance that what we hope for is going to happen. It is the evidence of things we cannot yet see" (Hebrews 11:1 NLT). It is a gift you can never grow out of. It never becomes old, worn, or out of style. With time, your faith in God will only become stronger and the world around you more beautiful and your challenges insignificant.

Should you ever feel you are losing your way and the burdens in your life seem overwhelming, remember to turn your thoughts to God and trust in His work in you. Read, study and apply God's word daily. Every day get into the habit of reading God's work, as easily as you would slip on your favorite outfit. At first, while you may find God's work to be two sizes too big or two sizes too small, the more accustomed you become to making it a part of your daily routine, the more you will find it has actually been designed to fit you like a glove. The trick is to learn how to wear it.

Never forget that even when you accept God's will and plan, life will test you, and there will be times when you struggle with your hope and feel abandoned by God. Should you ever find you are losing your way, and are overwhelmed with stress, take a moment to yourself and reconnect with your faith in God by saying the words of the Serenity Prayer.

The Serenity Prayer

God, grant me the Serenity
To accept the things I cannot change...
Courage to change the things I can,
And Wisdom to know the difference.
Living one day at a time,
Enjoying one moment at a time,
Accepting hardship as the pathway to peace.
Taking, as He did, this sinful world as it is,
Not as I would have it.
Trusting that He will make all things right
if I surrender to His will.
That I may be reasonably happy in this life,
And supremely happy with Him forever in the next.
Amen.
**Attributed to Reinhold Neibuhr

We all need serenity sometimes and the best way to calm our heart, mind and soul is to turn to God. You can turn to God through prayer, by reading His comforting word and promises in the Bible, or by simply taking the time to speak to Him in your thoughts and in your words. Be real with God when you talk to Him and listen to Him. Approach Him with thankfulness and adoration and praise in your own words.

Don't forget that the Bible is an excellent way for you to build your faith and get closer to God. Take the time to read about the many testaments of God's love for us – His children – and don't forget that you can approach and talk to God any time. He's always listening and waiting for you. When you talk to God, He will listen. When you cry on God's shoulder, He will give you comfort. When you tell your worries to God, He will help you overcome fear.

You need to understand that you are worthy of God's love. You are His child and He will never abandon you, no matter how much you try to push Him away. When you accept God into your life, and allow His spirit to find a home in your heart, know that He will never leave you, and He will be the light shining in the darkness that threatens your peace. Your faith in God makes you worthy of His love that comes with promises, and will help you recognize the powerful and beautiful being you are, so you can have faith in yourself and the abilities you have been given.

Remember, God can do everything in your life but fail, because He has done everything for the sake of the world, for the sake of humanity, and most importantly, for you. Nothing is too impossible for God. When God is your best friend you are never alone while here on earth.

About the Author

Robert Moment has a heart and love for people. Robert's life mission has been to reach God's people and offer hope, inspiration and support. As a business coach, speaker, and author he uses his God-given skills to encourage and inspire individuals to find and live their life's purpose. People need to be uplifted, healed and delivered! God has done all these things in his life. Robert wants God to be proud that He created him. He is passionate about empowering individuals to prosper and succeed, which is God's desire for your life. Robert is the CEO and Founder of The Moment Group, a business coaching and customer service consulting firm in Arlington, Virginia.

Robert's advice:

Operate in the fullness of God's Plan for Your Life.

Visit his websites:

www.customerservicetrainingskills.com

www.ChristianInspirational.org

"Think BIG and Embrace the Power of Possibilities"

--- Robert Moment

Author of God Will Always Be There For You

Volume Book Discounts

For information about special discounts for volume purchases of **God Will Always Be There For You** please contact Robert Moment at:

Email: Robert@ChristianInspirational.org

www.ingramcontent.com/pod-product-compliance
Lightning Source LLC
Chambersburg PA
CBHW071714040426
42446CB00011B/2058